MW00931665

Alcohol-Intused Recipes

Recipes

Everything You Need to Know About Cooking with Booze

BY

Daniel Humphreys

Copyright 2019 Daniel Humphreys

License Notes

No part of this Book can be reproduced in any form or by any means including print, electronic, scanning or photocopying unless prior permission is granted by the author.

All ideas, suggestions and guidelines mentioned here are written for informative purposes. While the author has taken every possible step to ensure accuracy, all readers are advised to follow information at their own risk. The author cannot be held responsible for personal and/or commercial damages in case of misinterpreting and misunderstanding any part of this Book

Table of Contents

Introduction

From appetizers to desserts, experience new tastes by cooking with booze.

Alcohol can be used to add flavor to dozens of dishes from Sizzling Sausages with Sherry to Caramelized Pineapple with Dark Rum.

There is a lot more to cooking with alcohol though, that merely splashing a shot or two in a pot or pan.

When used appropriately, beers, wines, and spirits can bring depth, richness, and flavor to sweet and savory dishes.

A Cookbook for Boozy Bakers will show you how to make the perfect Drunken Onion Soup, the ultimate Pan-Fried Venison with Sloe Gin Plum Sauce and the deliciously decadent Cherry Rum Balls.

Discover how to create restaurant quality food in your own kitchen by following our awesome cooking with booze recipes.

Whether you choose to cook with red wine, tequila or ouzo, our 40 recipes will teach you everything you need to learn about cooking with booze.

Appetizers

Apricot Brandy Brie

An easy appetizer that tastes extraordinary and is delicious served with strawberries and apple.

Portions: 6-8

Prep Time: 5mins

Cooking Time: 10mins

Total Time: 15mins

Ingredients:

- 1 (13.2 ounce) Brie wheel
- ½ cup apricot fruit jam
- ¼ cup brandy
- French bread (toasted)
- Fresh strawberries (washed, hulled, sliced)
- 1 green apple (finely sliced)

Directions:

1. Preheat the main oven to 350 degrees F.

2. Run a sharp knife around the top of the Brie wheel, approximately ¼" from its edge. Take care to only cut the rind. Make fine cuts across the surface and remove the top rind.

3. Place the Brie in a heatproof dish and bake in the oven for 12-15 minutes, or until the Brie begins to soften.

4. In the meantime, heat the apricot fruit jam using a saucepan over medium to low heat until it begins to bubble.

5. Turn off the heat and add the ¼ cup brandy. Stir well until incorporated. Carefully, pour the jam over the melted brie.

6. Serve the brie warm along with toasted French bread, a few fresh strawberries, and apple slices.

Beer Battered Asparagus with a Lemon Herb Dip

Asparagus spears battered in beer and served with a zesty dipping sauce makes a fantastic dinner party appetizer.

Portions: 2

Prep Time: 12mins

Cooking Time: 10mins

Total Time: 22mins

Ingredients:

Lemon Herb dipping sauce:

- ½ cup mayonnaise
- 1 tsp fresh lemon juice
- ½ tsp finely grated lemon zest
- ¼ tsp black pepper
- 1 tsp roughly chopped fresh thyme leaves
- ½ tsp roughly minced fresh rosemary leaves
- Pinch salt

Beer battered asparagus:

- Vegetable oil (for frying)
- 1 cup all-purpose flour
- 1 tsp salt
- 1 tsp pepper
- 1 tbsp. lemon zest (finely grated)
- 1 cup beer
- 1 pound asparagus spears (trimmed)

Directions:

1. To prepare the sauce; in a small bowl, combine all the sauce ingredients, cover and chill until ready to use.

2. To make the beer battered asparagus heat the vegetable oil in a large heavy saucepan until the temperature reaches 375 degrees F.

3. In a mixing bowl, whisk the flour together with the salt, pepper and lemon zest until combined.

4. Next, pour in the beer and whisk the ingredients until silky smooth.

5. Carefully, dip each piece of asparagus into the batter to evenly coat, shaking off any excess before you begin frying.

6. Transfer the battered asparagus to the oil and fry until golden brown, gently stir so that the asparagus doesn't stick together.

7. When cooked, place the asparagus on a kitchen paper towel-lined baking tray and keep warm in an oven set at 200 degrees F.

8. Serve with the dipping sauce on the side.

Bloody Mary and Pear Salad

A grown-up, warm salad that is as flavorsome as it is satisfying.

Portions: 4

Prep Time: 2mins

Cooking Time: N/A

Total Time: 2mins

Ingredients:

For the dressing:

- 1 fully ripe Anjou pear (cored, coarsely chopped)
- 1 cup low-sodium tomato juice
- 3 tbsp. lemon juice
- 3 tbsp. extra-virgin olive
- 3 tbsp. (80 proof) vodka
- ¼ cup English cucumber (unpeeled, chopped)
- 2 tsp horseradish (freshly grated)
- ½ tsp sea salt
- ½ tsp freshly ground black pepper
- ½ tsp hot pepper sauce
- ¼ tsp Worcestershire sauce

For the salad:

- 5 packed cups fresh baby spinach
- 4 slices whole-grain bread (toasted, diced)
- ¼ cup part-skim mozzarella cheese (shredded)
- 4 medium eggs (sunny side up)
- 8 sun-dried tomatoes (halved, no oil, rehydrated, thinly sliced)
- ¼ tsp smoked sea salt
- ¼ tsp freshly cracked black pepper

Directions:

1. Puree all of the dressing ingredients together in a food blender until silky smooth; this will take about 60 seconds.

2. In a large mixing bowl toss the spinach, together with the bread, cheese, and half of the vinaigrette. Arrange the salad on a serving platter. Top with sunny side up eggs and sun dried tomatoes. Season with salt and pepper.

3. Season and serve with the remaining vinaigrette on the side.

Carrot and Chestnut Soup with Wild Mushroom Confit

A sophisticated vegetable and nut soup served with a confit of wild mushrooms.

Portions: 6

Prep Time: 1hour 10mins

Cooking Time: 2hours 30mins

Total Time: 3hours 40mins

Ingredients:

- Water
- ½ cup dehydrated wild mushrooms
- Salt
- Pepper
- 2 tbsp. butter
- 1 tbsp. olive oil
- 2 shallots (chopped)
- 1 tbsp. garlic (minced)
- 4 carrots (chopped)
- 1 tsp ginger (chopped)
- 1 tsp turmeric
- 2 cups whole, peeled chestnuts in water (drained)
- ¼ cup brandy
- 3 cups low-sodium vegetable broth
- 1 tsp dried oregano
- 1 tbsp. thyme leaves (chopped)
- ½ cup light cream

Directions:

1. Preheat the main oven to 400 degrees F

2. To make the mushroom confit, in a small bowl filled with water, soak the mushrooms for 60 minutes.

3. Drain and use a kitchen paper towel to pat the mushrooms dry. Season well with salt and pepper and transfer to an aluminum foil-lined baking sheet. Bake in the oven for 1½ hours or until golden brown.

4. In the meantime, in a large pan over medium heat, melt the butter. Add the olive oil, shallots and minced garlic to the pan and fry until the garlic is browned, this will take 4-5 minutes.

5. Add the carrots along with the ginger, turmeric, chestnuts, and brandy. Reduce the heat to low and allow to reduce for 5-6 minutes. Next, add the broth, oregano, and thyme. Bring to a fast boil, before reducing the heat to low. Cover with a lid and simmer for 40-45 minutes until the carrots and chestnuts are just tender.

6. Allow to sit for 5 minutes before transferring to a food blender, process until the mixture is silky; this will take between 25-30 seconds.

7. Return the mixture to the pan, and season to taste.

8. Pour in the light cream and stir to combine.

9. Evenly divide the soup between 6 soup bowls and top with the comfit of mushroom.

Cheese and Prosecco Stuffed Zucchini Flowers

Cheese filled zucchini flowers stuffed with cheese and Prosecco are a more sophisticated twist on the usual stuffed vine leaves.

Portions: 2

Prep Time: 20mins

Cooking Time: 2mins

Total Time: 22mins

Ingredients:

- 4 zucchini flowers
- 14 ounces cream cheese
- 4 ounces Greek feta (crumbled)
- Pinch of thyme leaves
- Sunflower oil (for cooking)
- ½ a cup plain flour
- ½ cup Prosecco
- ¼ tsp salt
- Runny honey

Directions:

1. Lightly clean the zucchini flowers of dirt and insects by running them gently under cold running tap water. Take care not to soak the flowers. Pat dry with kitchen paper towels and using tweezers, remove the pollen parts of the flower (inside the base) along with the stamens.

2. In a mixing bowl, combine the cream cheese along with the Greek feta and thyme.

3. Using a teaspoon, carefully and evenly spoon the cheese mixture into the flowers. You will need to take care not the break the flowers.

4. Pour sufficient sunflower oil into a large, deep frying pan and heat. Ideally, the oil should be around 350 degrees F.

5. In the meantime, in a bowl mix together the flour, Prosecco, and salt. Whisk until the batter is lump free.

6. When the oil has reached its optimum temperature, carefully dip each stuffed zucchini flower in the batter. Shaking off any excess. Carefully, lower each battered flower into the hot oil and fry until the lower portion of each zucchini flower is crisp and golden brown, this will take around 60 seconds. Flip the flowers over and fry for a further 60 seconds until the other side is crisp and golden.

7. Using a slotted utensil, remove the flowers from the oil and drain off any excess oil using kitchen paper towel.

8. Drizzle with honey and serve.

Drunken French Onion Soup

A French onion, boozy soup served with toasted slices of bread and melted cheese.

Portions: 8

Prep Time: 15mins

Cooking Time: 1hour 8mins

Total Time: 1hour 23mins

Ingredients:

- 1 tbsp. olive oil
- 6 cups thinly sliced onions (thinly sliced)
- ½ pound baby portabella mushrooms (sliced)
- 1 tsp sugar
- 4 cloves garlic (peeled, sliced)
- ¼ cup sherry
- 1 tbsp. Dijon mustard
- ½ tsp dried thyme leaves
- 2 tbsp. all-purpose flour
- 6 cups low-sodium vegetable broth
- 1 cup dry white wine
- Salt and black pepper
- 1 French bread stick (sliced, toasted)
- 1 cup part-skim mozzarella cheese (shredded)
- ½ cup Parmesan cheese (grated)

Directions:

1. In a large frying pan or skillet over medium heat, heat the olive oil. When hot, sauté the sliced onions along with the mushrooms, constantly stirring until the onions are softened and golden brown, this will take around 12-15miutes.

2. Next, add the sugar and sliced garlic and continue cooking for 18-20 minutes, still stirring.

3. Pour in the sherry, constantly stirring to loosen any browned bits from the pan.

4. Stir in the Dijon mustard, dried thyme leaves and flour and stir for 60 seconds.

5. Add the vegetable broth and white wine. Bring to a fast boil, reduce heat to low and continue cooking for 25-30 minutes.

6. Taste and season accordingly.

7. Ladle the hot soup into ovenproof bowls, top with toasted French bread slice, scatter with shredded mozzarella and grated Parmesan.

8. Broil gently until the cheeses melt.

Jalapeno Hummus with Pale Ale

A spicy dip infused with pale ale to serve with potato chips or warm pita.

Portions: 2-4

Prep Time: 4mins

Cooking Time: N/A

Total Time: 4mins

Ingredients:

- 2 fresh jalapenos (stemmed, seeded, chopped)
- 3 tbsp. tahini
- 1½ cups garbanzo beans (drained, cooked)
- ⅓ cup cilantro (chopped)
- Juice of 1 fresh lime
- 1 tbsp. olive oil
- ½ tsp garlic powder
- ½ tsp salt
- ⅓ cup India Pale Ale
- ¼ tsp chili powder (optional)

Directions:

1. Add the first 8 ingredients (jalapeno through IPA) to a food blender and blitz until silky. You can add additional IPA if you require a thinner consistency dip.

2. For a spicier dip add ¼ teaspoon of chili powder.

3. Serve with warm pita.

Sambuca Shrimp

Enjoy this flambéed shrimp as an appetizer for four or a main course for two, served with rice.

Portions: 4

Prep Time: 3hours 5mins

Cooking Time: 10mins

Total Time: 3hours 15mins

Ingredients:

- 3 tbsp. butter (divided)
- 2 garlic cloves (minced)
- ½ cup heavy cream
- 1 pound jumbo cooked shrimp (thawed)
- 2 ounces Sambuca
- Salt and pepper

Directions:

1. First, in a small pan, melt 2 tablespoons of butter. Add to a mixing bowl along with the minced garlic and heavy cream. Stir well to combine.

2. Transfer the mixture to the refrigerator for 2-3 hours to allow the flavors to infuse.

3. In a heavy frying pan or skillet, melt the remaining butter on a medium to high heat and sauté the shrimp, until heated right through.

4. Pour in the Sambuca and flambé.

5. Reduce the heat and add the butter-cream mixture.

6. Simmer for 4-5 minutes and serve.

Sizzling Sausages with Sherry

A tempting tapas dish to share with friends over a glass of Rioja.

Portions: 10-12

Prep Time: 6mins

Cooking Time: 10mins

Total Time: 16mins

Directions:

- 1 ½ tsp olive oil
- 1 pound fresh pork link sausage (cut into 1 1/2" pieces)
- ⅓ cup dry Spanish sherry
- Flat leaf parsley (finely chopped)

Directions:

1. Heat the olive oil in a frying pan over medium heat. Add the sausages and cook for 4-5 minutes, or until brown on all sides.

2. Pour in the sherry and continue cooking on medium heat for a few minutes.

3. Remove from the pan and sprinkle with chopped parsley.

Smoked Salmon and Whiskey Spread

This whiskey spread is crying out to be generously spread onto hot, buttered brown toast.

Portions: 2 cups

Prep Time: 10mins

Cooking Time: N/A

Total Time: 8hours 20mins

Ingredients:

- 8 ounces cream cheese (softened)
- 2 ½ tbsp. whiskey
- 1 tbsp. fresh lemon juice
- ½ tsp ready-made horseradish
- 1½ tbsp. fresh dill (minced)
- 2 scallions (thinly sliced)
- 8 ounces smoked salmon (roughly chopped)

Directions:

1. In a medium-sized mixing bowl, combine the cream cheese along with the whiskey, fresh lemon juice, horseradish and minced dill. Beat well until the mixture is silky smooth.

2. Stir in the sliced scallions and salmon. Mix to incorporate.

3. Place the mixture in a small bowl and cover with a lid.

4. Transfer to the fridge overnight.

5. When you are ready to serve to allow the spread to rest at room temperature for 12-15 minutes, or until it becomes easy to spread.

6. Serve on hot, buttered brown toast.

Entrees

Beef Tenderloin with Mushrooms

This satisfying and yet elegant entrée is suitable for any occasion.

Portions: 4

Prep Time: 8mins

Cooking Time: 17mins

Total Time: 25mins

Ingredients:

- 4 beef tenderloin steaks (fat trimmed, cut ¾" thick)
- 1 tbsp. Dijon mustard
- 2 tbsp. olive oil
- 24 ounces Portobello mushrooms (sliced)
- ⅓ cup dry red wine
- 1 tbsp. Worcestershire sauce
- 2 tsp fresh thyme (snipped)

Directions:

1. Evenly spread each steak, on both sides, with Dijon mustard.

2. In a large frying pan or skillet, over medium to high heat, heat 1 tablespoon of olive oil.

3. Reduce the heat to medium and add the 4 steaks. Continue cooking, on both sides to preferred doneness.

4. Transfer the cooked steaks to a serving plate and keep warm.

5. Add the remaining olive oil to the frying pan drippings along with the mushrooms. Cook while stirring for 4 minutes.

6. Add the wine, together with the Worcestershire sauce and thyme. Leave uncovered and simmer for 3-4 minutes.

7. Ladle the sauce over the steaks.

Drunk Pasta Carbonara with Pomegranate Arils

A colorful and flavorsome way to serve pasta carbonara.

Portions: 4

Prep Time: 10mins

Cooking Time: 10mins

Total Time: 20mins

Ingredients:

- 12 ounces wheat beer
- 1½ cups chicken broth
- 12 ounces linguini
- 4 ounces pancetta (diced)
- 3 egg yolks
- 3 ounces Parmesan (shaved)
- ½ tsp salt
- 1 tsp pepper
- 1 cup baby arugula leaves
- ½ cup pomegranate arils

Directions:

1. Add the wheat beer along with the chicken broth to a large pot over medium heat and simmer.

2. Add the linguini and cook until nearly al dente. Drain the pasta, reserving about ¼ cup of the cooking liquid. Then transfer the pasta into a large bowl.

3. In a frying pan over medium to high heat add the diced pancetta, and cook until golden brown and crispy.

4. In a large bowl whisk the egg yolks along with the Parmesan, seasoning and the cooking liquid reserved earlier.

5. Pour the mixture over the linguini, tossing well to coat evenly.

6. Sprinkle the pancetta over the top of the pasta, scatter with arugula and arils.

Foil Barbecued Trout with Wine

A light and delicious dish. Lemon juice, fresh parsley and crisp white wine complement this delicate flakey fish perfectly.

Portions: 2

Prep Time: 15mins

Cooking Time: 20mins

Total Time: 35mins

Ingredients:

- 2 trout (cleaned, heads removed)
- ¼ cup dry white wine
- 2 tbsp. butter (melted)
- 1 tbsp. lemon juice
- 2 tbsp. fresh parsley (chopped)
- Salt and pepper

Directions:

1. Preheat the grill to medium to high heat.

2. On a flat, clean work surface lay out 2 pieces of aluminum foil of approximately 18" in length. Overlap them, so they make one very long and wide sheet.

3. Rinse the trout in cold water and using kitchen paper towels pat dry.

4. Arrange the trout in the middle of the foil, approximately 2-3" apart. Drizzle with white wine, melted butter, and lemon juice. Scatter with parsley and season well with salt and black pepper.

5. Fold the foil around the fish loosely, crimping the seams to seal the parcel. Place the fish parcel on the grill and cook for between 15-10 minutes, or until the trout is sufficiently cooked through and the fish flakes easily when using a fork.

Mussels in Irish Cream Whisky

It doesn't have to be St Patrick's Day, and you don't have to be in Galway to sample this traditional Irish dish, which is generally served with French fries.

Portions: 2

Prep Time: 7mins

Cooking Time: 13mins

Total Time: 20mins

Ingredients:

- 1 tbsp. onion (chopped)
- 2 scallions (chopped)
- 1 tbsp. leeks (chopped)
- Butter
- 1 pound Irish mussels (washed, cleaned)
- 1½ tbsp. white wine
- 2 tbsp. fish stock
- 1 tbsp. honey
- 1½ tbsp. Irish cream whiskey
- 2 tbsp. cream
- Sea salt
- ½ fresh lemon
- ½ bunch parsley

Directions:

1. In a large frying pan, heat and sweat the onions, scallion and leeks in 1-2 tablespoons of butter.

2. Add the mussels to the pan, along with the white wine and stock. Stir well to combine.

3. Add the honey, Irish cream, and cream. Bring to boil. Once boiling, reduce to a simmer and cook over moderate heat until all of the mussels have opened, for between 3-6 minutes. Remember to discard any unopened mussels.

4. Season well with sea salt and a squeeze of fresh lemon juice.

5. Garnish with chopped parsley and serve with crusty bread or French fries.

Ouzo Meatballs

Flavorsome ouzo infused meatballs to serve with rice, pasta or a green salad.

Portions: 4-6

Prep Time: 13mins

Cooking Time: 18mins

Total Time: 31mins

Ingredients:

- 1 medium onion (finely chopped)
- 2 tbsp. olive oil
- 1 pound 2 ounces ground beef
- 3 tbsp. bread crumbs
- 1 medium egg
- 1 tbsp. flour
- 1 tbsp. fresh parsley (chopped)
- 1 tbsp. fresh dill (chopped)
- 1 tbsp. fresh mint (chopped)
- 2 tbsp. ouzo
- 1 tsp each of salt and pepper
- ⅓ cup dry white wine

Directions:

1. In a frying pan sauté the onions in olive oil until golden brown.

2. In a mixing bowl combine all the ingredients along with the fried onions and using a food processor combine until incorporated.

3. Lightly grease a baking tin with oil

4. Lightly grease or dampen your hands and mold the mixture into balls of around 2".

5. Bake the balls, turning once or twice, on the baking tin under the grill for 12-15 minutes, or until cooked through and golden brown.

6. Serve.

Oysters Rockefeller

A classic New Orleans absinthe recipe created in 1899.

Portions: 4-6

Prep Time: 15mins

Cooking Time: 1hour

Total Time: 1hour 15mins

Ingredients:

- 4 pans rock salt
- 2 sticks butter (softened)
- ¾ cup cooked spinach (finely chopped)
- 6 tbsp. watercress leaves (very finely chopped)
- ¼ cup fresh scallion tops (finely chopped)
- 2 tbsp. celery (finely chopped)
- ¾ tsp salt
- ½ tsp white pepper
- ½ tsp dried marjoram
- ½ tsp dried basil
- ½ tsp cayenne
- ½ tsp ground anise seed
- ¼ cup absinthe
- 24 oysters on the half shell (drained)

Directions:

1. To make the sauce; in a stainless steel bowl, using a wooden spoon combine all the ingredients (excluding the oysters). Continue mixing, using a food blender at moderate speed.

2. Shape the sauce mixture into oval-shaped patties of around 2 ½ "x2"x1/2 "thick. You can do this by scooping out 2 tablespoons of sauce from the bowl and pressing it firmly into your palm.

3. Transfer the patties to a serving platter and place in the fridge while you get the oysters ready for baking.

4. To prepare the oysters first preheat the main oven to 500 degrees F.

5. First, thoroughly wash the oyster shells and pat dry.

6. Place an oyster on each shell and transfer them, in batches of 6, into each pan of rock salt.

7. Cover each oyster with a patty of sauce and bake for between 12-15 minutes, until the sauce begins to bubble and lightly browns on top.

8. Set aside to cool for 4-5 minutes before serving.

Pan-Fried Venison with Sloe Gin Plum Sauce

A luxurious meal for two served with an intensely fruity plum sauce. Serve with mashed potato and wilted spinach for a truly impressive dish.

Portions: 2

Prep Time: 20mins

Cooking Time: 20mins

Total Time: 40mins

Ingredients:

- 6 juniper berries (chopped)
- Black peppercorns
- 2 medium venison steaks
- 1 tbsp. sated butter
- 2 plums (pitted, quartered)
- 1 plum (pitted, quartered, finely chopped)
- 1 clove garlic (finely chopped)
- 3 tbsp. sloe gin
- 4 ounces hot beef broth
- Fresh thyme sprigs

Directions:

1. Firmly press the juniper berries and black peppercorns into each of the steaks.

2. Melt the butter in a skillet until foaming and then add the quarters of plums along with the venison steaks, flipping over halfway through cooking.

3. Remove the steaks and keep warm.

4. Add the chopped plums and chopped garlic into the pan juices. Cook, while stirring, until soft.

5. Add the gin and when sizzling, add the hot beef stock.

6. Once the plums are super soft, press the mixture through a sieve to remove the skins. Get the maximum amount of pulp possible as this adds flavor and thickness to the sauce. Add water if you need to dilute the sauce.

7. Transfer the steaks to warmed dinner plates, top with the cooked plum quarters and spoon on the sauce.

8. Sprinkle with thyme sprigs and black pepper.

9. Serve with mashed potato and wilted spinach.

Pork Loin with Champagne and Honey Glaze with Fried Spiced Apples

A delicious and decadent dish that is a dinner party winner guaranteed to impress family and friends.

Portions: 4

Prep Time: 50mins

Cooking Time: 40mins

Total Time: 1hour 30mins

Ingredients:

- 1½ cups Brut champagne
- 10½ ounces light brown sugar
- 3½ tsp clear honey
- ¾ tsp mustard powder
- ¾ tsp ground ginger
- 4 (8½ ounce) pork loin fillets
- 1 pinch each salt and black pepper
- 7 ounces butter

For the apples:

- 1⅓ sticks butter
- 2½ ounces sugar
- ¾ ounce ground allspice
- 4 medium green apples (cored, seeded, unpeeled, sliced)

Directions:

1. In a medium-sized saucepan add the Brut champagne along with the brown sugar, clear honey, mustard powder and ginger and bring to boil before simmering for 15 minutes.

2. Season the pork well with salt and black pepper.

3. In a frying pan melt the butter. Add the pork fillets and fry until golden brown, flipping over as it sizzles.

4. Add a generous spoonful of the glaze, swirl it around the pan for it to combine evenly with the butter. Continue adding more glaze, a small amount at a time.

5. Cook for approximately 15 minutes, or until the pork shines and the glaze becomes syrupy.

6. Put the pork to one side and keep it warm.

7. To prepare the apples, in a saucepan, melt the butter together with the sugar and ground allspice. Stir to combine and add the sliced apples.

8. Cook the apples for 4-5 minutes, or until they are soft and evenly coated in the glaze.

9. Serve immediately with the pork.

Salmon with Martini Sauce

It's time to get saucy with this salmon main course.

Portions: 4

Prep Time: 16mins

Cooking Time: 42mins

Total Time: 58mins

Ingredients:

- 2 cups dry vermouth
- ¼ cup shallots (minced)
- 2 tsp juniper berries (coarsely crushed)
- 1 tsp green peppercorns (coarsely crushed)
- 1 (8 ounce) bottle clam juice
- ¾ cup whipping cream
- 3 tbsp. salted butter
- 2 tsp virgin olive oil
- 4 (6 ounce) salmon fillets (boneless, skinless)
- 1 tbsp. fresh parsley (chopped)
- Salt and pepper
- ¼ cup pimiento-stuffed green olives (sliced)
- 2 tbsp. dry gin
- 2 tbsp. freshly squeezed lemon juice
- 1 tbsp. fresh chives (chopped)

Directions:

1. In a heavy medium-sized saucepan combine the dry vermouth along with the shallots, berries, and green peppercorns. Boil briskly until the liquid has reduced to only a ¼ cup, this will take around 10 minutes.

2. Pour in the clam juice and boil until reduced by half, for around 7 minutes.

3. Add the whipping cream and boil until the mixture is reduced to around ¾ cup, for 8 minutes.

4. Gradually, 1 tbsp. at a time, add the butter, as each addition of butter melts, add another but not before.

5. Strain the sauce through a mesh strainer. Return the sauce to the pan and keep warm until you are ready to serve.

6. In a large, heavy skillet over medium to high heat, heat the oil.

7. Sprinkle the salmon with chopped parsley and season with salt and pepper. Add the salmon to the skillet and sauté for 3-4 minutes each side, or until just cooked.

8. In the meantime, re-heat the sauce, if necessary and add the olives, gin and lemon juice, stirring to combine. Taste and season accordingly.

9. Arrange the salmon on dinner plates, drizzle with sauce and garnish with chopped chives.

Venison Steak in a Red Wine Chocolate Sauce

An entrée doesn't get much get more gourmet than tender venison steak served with a rich red wine chocolate sauce.

Portions: 4

Prep Time: 10mins

Cooking Time: 25mins

Total Time: 35mins

Ingredients:

Red wine chocolate sauce:

- 3 tbsp. butter
- 2 medium to large shallots (roughly chopped)
- 2 cloves garlic (roughly chopped)
- 1 sprig rosemary
- 1 tbsp. mixed peppercorns (crushed)
- 1½ cups Syrah red wine
- 4¼ cups beef stock
- ¼ cup dark 70% chocolate (finely grated)

Venison steaks:

- 4 (8 ounce) venison steaks
- 2 tbsp. mild flavored oil
- 2 tbsp. butter
- Salt and pepper

Directions:

1. To make the sauce, in a large pan, over medium heat, sauté in butter the chopped shallots, garlic, rosemary, and peppercorns until the shallots have just softened but haven't begun to caramelize; this will take between 4-5 minutes.

2. Add the Syrah red wine and reduce until the liquid has almost completely evaporated. Add the beef stock and reduce until the mixture is thick and saucy, this will take around 20 minutes.

3. In the meantime, while the sauce is reducing, cook the venison steaks.

4. To prepare the steaks; first, allow them to rest until they reach room temperature.

5. Season the steaks.

6. In a skillet heat the oil. As soon as it's warm, add the seasoned steaks and cook until either rare for 1-2 minutes per side or until medium rare for 3-4 minutes each side.

7. After flipping the venison steaks, add the butter, spooning it onto and over the steaks to baste them.

8. Transfer the steaks to a serving plate and allow them to rest for 1-2 minutes before slicing.

9. In the meantime, whisk the chocolate into the warm sauce, making sure that it doesn't boil.

10. Strain the chocolate sauce before serving.

Desserts

Amaretto Mousse Cheesecake

A no-bake Italian liqueur cheesecake for those oh, so special occasions.

Portions: 10-12

Prep Time: 5mins

Cooking Time: 10mins

Total Time: 8hours 15mins

Ingredients:

- 2 cups graham crackers (crumbed)
- ½ cup salted melted butter
- ½ cup cold water
- 1 (¼ ounce) pack unflavored gelatin
- 24 ounces cream cheese
- 1¼ cups white sugar
- 1 (5 ounce) can evaporated milk
- 1 tsp lemon juice
- ⅓ cup amaretto liqueur
- 1 tsp vanilla extract
- ¾ cup heavy whipping cream

Directions:

1. In a mixing bowl, combine the graham cracker crumbs along with the butter. Press the mixture into the base and the sides of a 9" springform cake tin and transfer to the refrigerator.

2. Pour the cold water into a saucepan and sprinkle with the unflavored gelatin. Allow the mixture to stand for 60 seconds. Stir the mixture over a low heat and when the gelatin has dissolved put to one side.

3. In a large mixing bowl beat the cream cheese along with the sugar until fluffy. A little at a time, add the milk and lemon juice and continue beating until the mixture is a fluffy consistency. Scrape down the sides and bottom of the bowl to make sure no lumps remain.

4. Add the amaretto and vanilla extract together with the gelatin mixture and beat until incorporated.

5. In another bowl, whip the cream until stiff. Fold the whipped cream into the cream cheese mixture.

6. Pour the filling into the crust and transfer to the refrigerator overnight.

7. When you are ready to serve remove the springform tin.

Bananas Foster

An iconic, creamy rum flavored dessert from pan to plate in just 20 minutes.

Portions: 4

Prep Time: 5mins

Cooking Time: 15mins

Total Time: 20mins

Ingredients:

- ¼ cup butter
- ⅔ cup dark brown sugar
- 3½ tbsp. rum
- 1½ tsp vanilla extract
- ½ tsp ground cinnamon
- 3 bananas (peeled, sliced lengthwise and crosswise)
- ¼ cup walnuts (coarsely chopped)
- 1 pint vanilla ice cream

Directions:

1. In a deep frying pan or skillet over medium heat, melt the butter.

2. Stir in the dark brown sugar along with the rum, vanilla extract, and ground cinnamon.

3. As soon as the mixture starts to bubble, add the bananas and chopped walnuts.

4. Continue cooking for 1-2 minutes or until the bananas are heated through.

5. Serve over ice cream.

Caramelized Pears with Rum Butter Sauce

A rich rum butter sauce served over warm, ripe pears make a simple yet sophisticated dessert.

Portions: 4

Prep Time: 5mins

Cooking Time: 15mins

Total Time: 20mins

Ingredients:

- Rum Butter Sauce:
- ½ cup brown sugar
- ½ cup unsalted butter
- ½ cup heavy whipping cream
- ¼ cup spiced rum

Pears:

- 1 tbsp. unsalted butter
- 4 ripe pears (quartered)
- 1 quart vanilla ice cream
- Fresh mint (to garnish)

Directions:

1. To make the butter sauce combine all 4 sauce ingredients in a small pan and over low heat, heat until the mixture begins to bubble. Continue cooking over medium to low heat on a simmer for 4-5 minutes until the sauce begins to thicken.

2. Remove the pan from the heat and allow to cool.

3. To prepare the pears, add the unsalted butter to a frying pan over medium heat. As soon as the butter melts add the pears, and cook for a few minutes each side, until the pears begin to caramelize.

4. Serve the pears warm with a generous scoop of vanilla ice cream.

5. Garnish with fresh mint.

Caramelized Pineapple with Dark Rum

One taste of this rum infused dessert, and you will be transported to the Caribbean.

Portions: 2

Prep Time: 10mins

Cooking Time: 10mins

Total Time: 25mins

Ingredients:

- 1 large, ripe pineapple
- 2 tbsp. unsalted butter
- 3 tbsp. packed dark brown sugar
- 2 tbsp. dark rum
- Ice cream (to serve)

Directions:

1. Preheat your broiler. Line a shallow baking pan with aluminum foil

2. First, prepare the pineapple by trimming the leaves to around 2". Next, quarter the pineapple lengthwise, setting two quarters aside for an alternative use.

3. Cut and discard the cores from the remaining two quarters and using a sharp knife cut the fruit away from the rind while taking care to keep the rinds intact. Set aside. Finally, cut the pineapple crosswise into 1/4 "thick slices.

4. In a medium saucepan, over medium heat, cook the butter along with 2 tablespoons of dark brown sugar and dark rum, stirring for 60 seconds. Add the pineapple, stirring for 60 seconds to make sure that the mixture coats the fruit.

5. Place the reserved rinds in the baking pan and using a spoon and fork return the pineapple fruit to the rinds; attempting to return the pineapple to its original shape.

6. Spoon the remaining butter mixture over the fruit and sprinkle with the remaining dark brown sugar.

7. Broil the pineapple approximately 3-4" away from the heat until just charred and sufficiently heated; this will take between 7-8 minutes.

8. Serve with a large dollop of ice cream.

Cherry Rum Balls

Decadent little rum balls filled with sweet, candied cherries.

Portions: 24

Prep Time: 15mins

Cooking Time: N/A

Total Time: 15mins

Ingredients:

- 1 cup semisweet chocolate chips (melted)
- ½ cup rum

- ¼ cup light corn syrup
- 3 cups vanilla wafer crumbs
- 1½ cups pecan (chopped)
- 1 cup confectioner's sugar
- 24 red candied cherries (halved)

Directions:

1. In a bowl combine the melted chocolate chips with the rum and corn syrup.

2. In a second bowl combine the vanilla wafer crumbs along with the chopped pecans and half of the confectioner's sugar

3. Drizzle the chocolate-rum mixture over the crumb mixture and stir until incorporated.

4. Using clean fingers form the mixture into 1" ball shapes. Roll each ball in the remaining sugar.

5. Arrange a cherry half in the middle of each ball, and using the back of a fork press down on the ball very gently.

6. Store in an airtight, lidded container for a few days before enjoying.

Drunken Monkey Bread

Brandy adds killer taste to this spiced monkey bread.

Portions: 8-10

Prep Time: 20mins

Cooking Time: 1hour

Total Time: 14hours 20mins

Ingredients:

- 3 pounds frozen bread dough *
- Cooking spray
- Butter
- 1 cup granulated sugar
- 1 tbsp. pumpkin spice
- 2 ½ sticks melted butter
- ¾ cup brown sugar
- ¼ cup brandy

Zest of 1 orange

Directions:

1. Place the frozen dough on a parchment-lined baking sheet. Lightly mist a large piece of plastic wrap with cooking spray and place it over the dough to completely cover.

2. Set the dough aside to rise according to package directions; this should take between 3-5 hours.

3. As soon as the dough has increased to two or three times its size, butter a 12-15 cup bundt pan.

4. In a mixing bowl combine the sugar along with the pumpkin spice. Using kitchen scissors snip the dough into 1-1 ½ "pieces.

5. Lightly dust each piece with the sugar mixture and transfer it to the bundt pan. Cover the pan and place it in the fridge overnight.

6. Position the oven rack on the bottom shelf and remove the remaining racks to allow the monkey bread to rise.

7. Preheat the main oven to 375 degrees F.

8. In a microwave-safe bowl, whisk the melted butter along with the brown sugar, brandy, and orange zest. Heat the mixture to boiling point in the microwave for 2 minutes.

9. Pour the mixture over the monkey dough and place in the preheated oven. Bake for between 45-60 minutes, or until the top is crusty and browned and rising over the top of the bundt pan.

*Not the partially baked variety

Fresh Peaches with Amaretto Sauce

Sweet fresh peaches served with a rich almond flavor amaretto sauce.

Portions: 4

Prep Time: 10mins

Cooking Time: 1hour

Total Time: 1hour 10mins

Ingredients:

- 2 tbsp. sugar
- 1 tbsp. cornstarch
- 1 cup soymilk
- 1 tbsp. amaretto liqueur
- 1 tsp vanilla
- 4 cups peaches (pitted, sliced)

Directions:

1. In a stainless steel pan combine the sugar along with the cornstarch and using a whisk, whisk in the soymilk and amaretto until incorporated.

2. Bring to boil over medium heat, while constantly stirring for 60 seconds. Remove from the heat and add the vanilla. Stir to combine.

3. Transfer to the refrigerator for 1-2 hours, or until totally chilled.

4. Evenly divide the peaches between 4 dessert bowls.

5. Spoon lots of amaretto sauce over the peaches and serve.

Shortbread Bars with Whisky Marmalade

Buttery shortbread squares with sweet whiskey marmalade are perfect served with after dinner coffee.

Portions: 20

Prep Time: 10mins

Cooking Time: 45mins

Total Time: 55mins

Ingredients:

- 7¾ ounces butter
- 1 ounce icing sugar
- 2¾ ounces caster sugar
- Zest of 1 orange
- 1 ounce corn flour
- 10½ ounces flour
- 1 cup marmalade
- 3 tsp whiskey
- Icing sugar (to dust)

Directions:

1. Preheat the main oven to 325 degrees F. Line a 10x6" baking tin with parchment paper.

2. Using a mixer, preferably electric, beat the butter along with the icing sugar. Add the caster sugar and orange zest and beat to combine.

3. Gradually sift in the cornflour and the flour and mix on a low setting until a coarse crumb consistency is achieved.

4. Transfer 75% of the coarse crumb dough mixture into the baking tin and evenly spread it around the bottom of the tin; without pressing down hard. Using a fork, prick the mixture lots of times.

5. In a bowl, combine the marmalade with the whiskey, stir well and evenly spread this on top of the shortbread crumb.

6. Crumble the remaining 25% of the dough over the top and bake in the oven for between 40-45 minutes, or until the crumb is just golden.

7. Chop into squares while warm and set to one side to completely cool.

8. Dust with icing sugar before serving.

Sorbet à l'absinthe

A refreshing palate cleanser to enjoy in between courses and this recipe was served in honor of Gustave Eiffel's Parisian tower in 1889.

Portions: 4-6

Prep Time: 6mins

Cooking Time: 10mins

Total Time: 4hours 16mins

Ingredients:

- 17 ounces cold water
- 10½ ounces sugar
- ¾ ounce fresh absinthe leaves
- Juice of 1 orange and 1 lemon
- 3⅓ ounces absinthe*

Directions:

1. First, make the syrup by blending 8½ ounces of cold water along with the sugar over a low heat for 10 minutes. Next, infuse the fresh absinthe leaves in the syrup. Set to one side to cool.

2. Remove the absinthe leaves and add both the orange and lemon juice, along with the remaining water. Transfer to the freezer to set.

3. Before serving, allow the sorbet to soften a little before adding the absinthe.

*Absinthe can be sourced online

White Rum and Chocolate Tropical Trifle

A beautifully fruity trifle full to bursting with mango, banana and passion fruit spiked with a healthy dose of rum.

Portions: 10

Prep Time: 45mins

Cooking Time: 20mins

Total Time: 9hours 5mins

Ingredients:

- 10 ounces butter cake (chopped into cubes)
- ¼ cup white rum
- Pulp from 2 passion fruits (peeled, chopped)
- 1 pound white chocolate melts
- 1¾ cups heavy cream
- ¼ cup light brown sugar
- 1 pound mango (peeled, chopped)
- 2 bananas (peeled, sliced)
- 3 passion fruits, (peeled, chopped)
- 2 cups whipped thickened cream
- Shredded coconut (shredded for garnish)

Directions:

1. Arrange the pieces of cake in the bottom of a shallow 3 quart serving dish.

2. Combine the white rum with the passion fruit pulp and drizzle over the cake.

3. In a double boiler, gently melt the white chocolate.

4. Using a medium saucepan gently warm the cream and brown sugar. It needs to be lukewarm rather than hot.

5. Pour the cream into the melted chocolate, whisking to combine. Pour the mixture over the cake and passion fruit pulp and transfer to the refrigerator to set.

6. Spoon the chopped fruit over the chocolate, dollop the whipped cream on top, scatter with shredded coconut and chill overnight.

Sides and Sauces

Absinthe BBQ Sauce

A small amount of absinthe gives the sauce a delicate aniseed flavor. Serve the sauce on a burger with fried onions, cheese and bacon - it's incredible.

Portions: 2-4

Prep Time: 25mins

Cooking Time: 27mins

Total Time: 52mins

Ingredients:

- 6 cloves garlic (minced)
- 1 yellow onion (grilled, chopped)
- 1 green bell pepper (grilled, chopped)
- 3 ribs celery (grilled, chopped)
- 4 ounces tomato paste
- 1 cup brown sugar
- 32 ounces tomato juice
- 1 cup Worcestershire sauce
- ½ cup hot sauce
- ½ cup raisins
- 2 ounces absinthe*
- 2 ounces sugarcane vinegar

Directions:

1. First, in a medium-size saucepan, over medium heat, sauté the garlic until browned. Add the grilled vegetables and continue to sauté for a further 60 seconds.

2. Add the tomato paste to the pan along with the brown sugar, and cook while stirring for 4-5 minutes. Pour in the tomato juice, Worcestershire sauce, hot sauce, and raisins and simmer for 18-20 minutes.

3. Remove the pan from the heat, taste and season accordingly. Allow the mixture to cool slightly before transferring it to a food blender. On a high setting puree the mixture.

4. Strain the puree into a small pan and add the absinthe and sugarcane vinegar. Gently warm before serving.

*Absinthe can be sourced online

Baked Beans Bourbon Style

Jazz up your baked beans with coffee and bourbon.

Portions: 4

Prep Time: 3mins

Cooking Time: 1hour

Total Time: 1hour 3mins

Ingredients:

- 2 (28 ounce) cans baked beans
- ½ cup chili sauce
- ½ cup strong coffee
- ¼ cup bourbon
- 3 tsp dry mustard

Directions:

1. Preheat the main oven to 350 degrees F.

2. In a mixing bowl combine all 5 ingredients and stir to incorporate.

3. Transfer to a 2 quart casserole dish and bake for 60 minutes, or until beginning to bubble.

Bloody Mary Cherry Tomatoes with Pepper Salt

Enjoy as a side, an hors-d'oeuvres or a picnic bite.

Portions: 60

Prep Time: 45mins

Cooking Time: 3secs

Total Time: 1hour 45mins 3secs

Ingredients:

- 3 pints firm small mixed cherry and grape tomatoes
- ½ cup vodka
- 3 tbsp. white wine vinegar
- 1 tbsp. superfine granulated sugar
- 1 tsp grated lemon zest
- 3 tbsp. kosher salt
- 1½ tbsp. coarsely ground black pepper

Directions:

1. Using a sharp knife cut a tiny cross in the bottom of each tomato. In a medium pan of boiling water, blanch the tomatoes, only five at time for 3 seconds. Transfer them straight away using a slotted spoon to an ice bath. (This will prevent them from cooking any more).

2. Drain the tomatoes and peel before placing them in a shallow dish.

3. In a mixing bowl combine the vodka along with the white vinegar, sugar and lemon zest. Stir until the sugar has dissolved.

4. Pour the mixture over the tomatoes, gently tossing them to coat evenly.

5. Transfer them to the refrigerator to marinate for 60 minutes.

6. Season with kosher salt and black pepper before serving.

Creamy Malibu Coconut Dipping Sauce

The perfect dipping sauce to serve with jumbo shrimp.

Portions: 4-5*

Prep Time: 5mins

Cooking Time: N/A

Total Time: 5mins

Ingredients:

- 4 tbsp. sour cream
- 1 ½ tbsp. mayonnaise
- ¼ lime (freshly squeezed)
- 2 tbsp. coconut (shredded)
- 1 ½ tbsp. honey
- 1 tbsp. Malibu Rum
- 1 dash garlic powder
- Cracked black pepper – to taste
- ½ cup pineapple (peeled, chopped, finely crushed)

Directions:

1. Combine the first 8 ingredients in a mixing bowl and using whisk to incorporate.

2. Add the crushed pineapple and stir to combine.

3. Whisk together to evenly distribute ingredients.

4. Serve.

*There will be sufficient sauce for around 20 shrimps

Drunken Fruit Salsa

Served this fruity salsa with grilled meat or fish and rice.

Portions: 6

Prep Time: 15mins

Cooking Time: N/A

Total Time: 3hours 15mins

Ingredients:

- 1 medium mango (peeled, finely diced)
- ¾ cup fresh strawberries (chopped)
- 1 kiwi (peeled, finely diced)
- 1 jalapeno pepper (seeded, finely chopped)
- 2 tbsp. fresh mint (chopped)
- ¼ cup rum

Directions:

1. In a glass mixing bowl or large dish combine all the ingredients. Stir well to incorporate.

2. Transfer to the refrigerator for 2-3 hours, stirring every 45 minutes or so.

Gin and Lime Marmalade Jam

Serve this marmalade on ice cream, fruit or toasted bread or why not give a jar to a friend this Christmas. This marmalade makes the perfect edible gift.

Portions: 4*

Prep Time: 15mins

Cooking Time: 2hours

Total Time: 2hours 15mins

Ingredients:

- 2 medium lemons
- 9 medium limes
- 8 cups cold water
- 10 lime leaves
- 3⅓ pounds white sugar
- 4 tbsp. gin

Directions:

1. First, juice the citrus fruit, use a spoon to scrape out the pulp along with the seeds. Using a fine sieve strain the juice, and put the pulp and seeds to one side. Pour the juice into a measuring jug and top up with water to make 2 quarts.

2. Put the pulp together with the seeds in a clean piece of muslin, and tie with kitchen strip to make a parcel.

3. Using a sharp knife finely shred the lemon and lime rinds and place into a large pot along with the 2 quarts of juice, lime leaves, and the muslin parcel.

4. Bring the pot to a boil. Gently simmer for 60 minutes, or until the peel becomes translucent and soft.

5. Remove the muslin parcel from the pot.

6. Gently warm the sugar on a baking sheet in an oven at 320 degrees F, for 5 minutes.

7. Add the sugar to the marmalade mixture and gently simmer for 45-50 minutes. Test if the marmalade is sufficiently cooked by spooning a small amount onto a chilled plate and putting it in the refrigerator for 2-3 minutes; it's ready when a surface skin forms.

8. Add 1 tablespoon of gin to 4 (4-pound) jam jars, and spoon in the hot marmalade mixture.

9. Seal, invert the jars and put to one side to completely cool.

*Makes 4 (4-pound) jars of marmalade

Orange Liqueur Mango Sauce

A sensationally sweet sauce to serve with fruit, sorbet or over ice cream.

Portions: 2 (1 cup)

Prep Time: 4mins

Cooking Time: 3mins

Total Time: 7mins

Ingredients:

- 3 tbsp. sugar
- 3 tbsp. cold water
- 2 mangoes (peeled, pitted, chopped)
- 2 tbsp. orange liqueur

Directions:

1. In a small-sized saucepan, combine the sugar along with the water.

2. Cook over medium heat for 2-3 minutes, or until sugar is totally dissolved.

3. In a food blender, process the syrup, together with the chopped mangos and the orange liqueur until silky smooth.

4. Transfer to a covered container and refrigerate for up to 72 hours.

Port and Cheese Dip

A sophisticated dip best served with slices of green apple dipped in fresh lemon juice.

Portions: 6

Prep Time: 5mins

Cooking Time: N/A

Total Time: 8 hours 5mins

Ingredients:

- ½ pound Imperial cheddar cheese (cold pack)
- ½ cup sour cream
- ¼ cup port wine

Directions:

1. Crumble the cheese.

2. In a mixing bowl beat the crumbled cheese together with the sour cream and port wine.

3. Transfer to a container with a tight lid and chill in the refrigerator overnight.

Sautéed Sherry Mushrooms

A side order of sherry and mushrooms is sublime served with steak.

Portions: 2cups

Prep Time: 5mins

Cooking Time: 20mins

Total Time: 25mins

Ingredients:

- Olive oil

- 1½ pounds button mushrooms (washed, dried, quartered)
- ½ cup dry sherry
- Sea salt and freshly ground black pepper

Directions:

1. Lightly coat a large frying pan or skillet with olive oil and place over high heat.

2. Add the button mushrooms and fry until they have significantly reduced in size, and are beginning to brown, while occasionally stirring. This will take around 8-10 minutes.

3. Reduce the heat and using the dry sherry deglaze the frying pan. Increase the heat to high and using a wooden flat edged spatula gently loosen any bits of mushroom from the surface of the pan.

4. Continue cooking until the liquid has completely evaporated and season well.

5. Serve as a side with steak.

Sriracha Beer Butter Grilled Corn

Beer butter grilled corn compliments so many dishes including burgers, ribs, steak, and chicken.

Portions: 6

Prep Time: 7mins

Cooking Time: 8mins

Total Time: 1 hour 15mins

Ingredients:

- ½ cup cold butter (cubed)
- 3 tbsp. India pale ale beer
- 1 tsp sriracha hot sauce
- ½ tsp garlic powder
- ¼ tsp salt
- 6 ears corn (shucked)
- 2 tbsp. olive oil
- Salt and black pepper
- ¼ cup fresh cilantro (chopped)

Directions:

1. In a food processor, and using a paddle attachment beat the unsalted butter until fluffy.

2. Add the pale ale along with the sriracha, garlic powder, and kosher salt and beat until incorporated.

3. Transfer the butter to a sheet of plastic wrap, tightly roll into a log shape and place in the refrigerator for 60 minutes to set.

4. Preheat your grill.

5. Brush the fresh corn with oil and season with salt and black pepper.

6. Grill the corn, turning every once in a while, until tender and charred, this will take 7-10 minutes.

7. Transfer the grilled corn to an aluminum foil-lined serving plate, top with lots of butter and sprinkle with chopped cilantro.

Author's Afterthoughts

Thanks ever so much to each of my cherished readers for investing the time to read this book!

I know you could have picked from many other books but you chose this one. So, a big thanks for downloading this book and reading all the way to the end.

If you enjoyed this book or received value from it, I'd like to ask you for a favor. Please take a few minutes to post an honest and heartfelt review on Amazon.com. Your support does make a difference and helps to benefit other people.

Thanks!

Daniel Humphreys

About The Author

Daniel Humphreys

Many people will ask me if I am German or Norman, and my answer is that I am 100% unique! Joking aside, I owe my cooking influence mainly to my mother who was British! I can certainly make a mean Sheppard's pie, but when it comes to preparing Bratwurst sausages and drinking beer with friends, I am also all in!

I am taking you on this culinary journey with me and hope you can appreciate my diversified background. In my 15 years career as a chef, I never had a dish returned to me by one of clients, so that should say something about me! Actually, I will take that back. My worst critic is my four years old son, who refuses to taste anything that is green color. That shall pass, I am sure.

My hope is to help my children discover the joy of cooking and sharing their creations with their loved ones, like I did all my life. When you develop a passion for cooking and my suspicious is that you have one as well, it usually sticks for life. The best advice I can give anyone as a professional chef is invest. Invest your time, your heart in each meal you are creating. Invest also a little money in good cooking hardware and quality ingredients. But most of all enjoy every meal you prepare with YOUR friends and family!

Made in the USA
Las Vegas, NV
12 November 2024

11705975R00073